W0018926

THIS NOTEBOOK BELONGS TO

....

Clarkson Potter/Publishers
New York

READING CHECKLIST

- [ ] *After Dark* by Haruki Murakami (2004)
- [ ] *Altered Carbon* by Richard K. Morgan (2002)
- [ ] *The Black Dahlia* by James Ellroy (1987)
- [ ] *Black Leopard Red Wolf* by Marlon James (2019)
- [ ] *Black Light* by Kimberly King Parsons (2019)
- [ ] *Black Water Rising* by Attica Locke (2009)
- [ ] *Coal River* by Ellen Marie Wiseman (2015)
- [ ] *Cosmos* by Carl Sagan (1980)
- [ ] *A Feast for Crows* by George R. R. Martin (2005)
- [ ] *The Left Hand of Darkness* by Ursula Le Guin (1969)
- [ ] *The Man in the Iron Mask* by Alexandre Dumas (1839)
- [ ] *Midnight's Children* by Salman Rushdie (1981)
- [ ] *Mother Night* by Kurt Vonnegut (1961)
- [ ] *Nightwood* by Djuna Barnes (1936)
- [ ] *Oil!* by Upton Sinclair (1926)
- [ ] *The Raven* by Edgar Allan Poe (1845)
- [ ] *A Scanner Darkly* by Philip K. Dick (1977)
- [ ] *The Starless Sea* by Erin Morgenstern (2019)
- [ ] *Tree of Smoke* by Denis Johnson (2007)
- [ ] *Washington Black* by Esi Edugyan (2018)

Published in the United States by Clarkson Potter/
Publishers, an imprint of Random House, a division
of Penguin Random House LLC, New York.
clarksonpotter.com

CLARKSON POTTER is a trademark and POTTER
with colophon is a registered trademark of Penguin
Random House LLC.

ISBN 978-1-9848-2611-4

Printed in Malaysia

Book and cover design by Jessie Kaye

10 9 8 7 6 5 4 3 2 1

First Edition

THIS NOTEBOOK BELONGS TO

―――――――――――――――――――――――――――――――

Clarkson Potter/Publishers
New York

READING CHECKLIST

- [ ] *The Camomile Lawn* by Mary Wesley (1984)
- [ ] *Fried Green Tomatoes at the Whistle Stop Cafe* by Fannie Flagg (1987)
- [ ] *Girl with Green Eyes* by Edna O'Brien (1962)
- [ ] *Gods of Jade and Shadow* by Silvia Moreno-Garcia (2019)
- [ ] *Gold Boy, Emerald Girl* by Yiyun Li (2010)
- [ ] *The Grass Is Singing* by Doris Lessing (1950)
- [ ] *Grasshopper Jungle* by Andrew Smith (2014)
- [ ] *The Green House* by Mario Vargas Llosa (1966)
- [ ] *The Green Mile* by Stephen King (1996)
- [ ] *The Green Road* by Anne Enright (2015)
- [ ] *Into the Forest* by Jean Hegland (1996)
- [ ] *Leaves of Grass* by Walt Whitman (1855)
- [ ] *Little Pea* by Amy Krouse Rosenthal (2005)
- [ ] *The Miracle Life of Edgar Mint* by Brady Udall (2001)
- [ ] *Olive Kitteridge* by Elizabeth Strout (2008)
- [ ] *Seaweed Chronicles* by Susan Hand Shetterly (2018)
- [ ] *Stalking the Wild Asparagus* by Euell Gibbons (1962)
- [ ] *Through the Arc of the Rain Forest* by Karen Tei Yamashita (1990)
- [ ] *Under the Greenwood Tree* by Thomas Hardy (1872)
- [ ] *The Witch of Lime Street* by David Jaher (2015)

Published in the United States by Clarkson Potter/
Publishers, an imprint of Random House, a division
of Penguin Random House LLC, New York.
clarksonpotter.com

CLARKSON POTTER is a trademark and POTTER
with colophon is a registered trademark of Penguin
Random House LLC.

ISBN 978-1-9848-2611-4

Printed in Malaysia

Book and cover design by Jessie Kaye

10 9 8 7 6 5 4 3 2 1

First Edition

THIS NOTEBOOK BELONGS TO

Clarkson Potter/Publishers
New York

READING CHECKLIST

- [ ] *American Rust* by Philipp Meyer (2009)
- [ ] *An American Sunrise* by Joy Harjo (2019)
- [ ] *Bark* by Lorrie Moore (2014)
- [ ] *The Bronze Bow* by Elizabeth George Speare (1961)
- [ ] *Brown Girl, Brownstones* by Paule Marshall (1959)
- [ ] *The Carrot Seed* by Ruth Krauss (1945)
- [ ] *The Chestnut Man* by Søren Sveistrup (2018)
- [ ] *A Clockwork Orange* by Anthony Burgess (1962)
- [ ] *The Copper Beech* by Maeve Binchy (1992)
- [ ] *The Coral Sea* by Patti Smith (1996)
- [ ] *Dragonfly in Amber* by Diana Gabaldon (1992)
- [ ] *Five Quarters of the Orange* by Joanne Harris (2000)
- [ ] *The Ginger Man* by J.P. Donleavy (1955)
- [ ] *The House on Mango Street* by Sandra Cisneros (1984)
- [ ] *James and the Giant Peach* by Roald Dahl (1961)
- [ ] *Like Water for Chocolate* by Laura Esquivel (1989)
- [ ] *The Mandarins* by Simone de Beauvoir (1954)
- [ ] *Norwegian Wood* by Haruki Murakami (1987)
- [ ] *Portrait in Sepia* by Isabel Allende (2000)
- [ ] *Sunset Song* by Lewis Grassic Gibbon (1932)

Published in the United States by Clarkson Potter/
Publishers, an imprint of Random House, a division
of Penguin Random House LLC, New York.
clarksonpotter.com

CLARKSON POTTER is a trademark and POTTER
with colophon is a registered trademark of Penguin
Random House LLC.

ISBN 978-1-9848-2611-4

Printed in Malaysia

Book and cover design by Jessie Kaye

10 9 8 7 6 5 4 3 2 1

First Edition

THIS NOTEBOOK BELONGS TO

.
_____

Clarkson Potter/Publishers
New York

READING CHECKLIST

- [ ] *Almost Transparent Blue* by Ryu Murakami (1976)
- [ ] *Aquamarine* by Alice Hoffman (2001)
- [ ] *Black and Blue* by Anna Quindlen (1998)
- [ ] *Blue Bloods* by Melissa de la Cruz (2006)
- [ ] *The Bluest Eye* by Toni Morrison (1970)
- [ ] *Bluets* by Maggie Nelson (2009)
- [ ] *Devil in a Blue Dress* by Walter Mosley (1990)
- [ ] *The Girl of Ink and Stars* by Kiran Millwood Hargrave (2016)
- [ ] *The House in the Cerulean Sea* by T. J. Klune (2020)
- [ ] *The Lake House* by Kate Morton (2015)
- [ ] *The Ocean at the End of the Lane* by Neil Gaiman (2013)
- [ ] *The Prince of Tides* by Pat Conroy (1986)
- [ ] *The Sheltering Sky* by Paul Bowles (1949)
- [ ] *So Much Blue* by Percival Everett (2017)
- [ ] *A Spool of Blue Thread* by Anne Tyler (2015)
- [ ] *Storm of Steel* by Ernst Jünger, translated by Michael Hofmann (1920)
- [ ] *The Turquoise Ledge* by Leslie Marmon Silko (2010)
- [ ] *The Water Dancer* by Ta-Nehisi Coates (2019)
- [ ] *The Weary Blues* by Langston Hughes (1926)
- [ ] *Wide Sargasso Sea* by Jean Rhys (1966)

Published in the United States by Clarkson Potter/
Publishers, an imprint of Random House, a division
of Penguin Random House LLC, New York.
clarksonpotter.com

CLARKSON POTTER is a trademark and POTTER
with colophon is a registered trademark of Penguin
Random House LLC.

ISBN 978-1-9848-2611-4

Printed in Malaysia

Book and cover design by Jessie Kaye

10 9 8 7 6 5 4 3 2 1

First Edition

THIS NOTEBOOK BELONGS TO

_____

Clarkson Potter/Publishers
New York

READING CHECKLIST

- [ ] *Alone in the Kitchen with an Eggplant* by Jenni Ferrari-Adler (2007)
- [ ] *Beyond Magenta* by Susan Kuklin (2014)
- [ ] *Blackberry Wine* by Joanne Harris (2000)
- [ ] *Children of the Jacaranda Tree* by Sahar Delijani (2013)
- [ ] *The Color Purple* by Alice Walker (1982)
- [ ] *Dark Elderberry Branch* by Marina Tsvetaeva (1923)
- [ ] *Djinn Patrol on the Purple Line* by Deepa Anappara (2020)
- [ ] *Empress Orchid* by Anchee Min (2003)
- [ ] *Fig* by Sarah Elizabeth Schantz (2015)
- [ ] *The Grapes of Wrath* by John Steinbeck (1939)
- [ ] *The Lavender Garden* by Lucinda Riley (2012)
- [ ] *March Violets* by Philip Kerr (1989)
- [ ] *Mauve Desert* by Nicole Brossard (1987)
- [ ] *Purple Hibiscus* by Chimamanda Ngozi Adichie (2003)
- [ ] *Redemption in Indigo* by Karen Lord (2010)
- [ ] *Riders of the Purple Sage* by Zane Grey (1912)
- [ ] *Save Me the Plums* by Ruth Reichl (2019)
- [ ] *Twilight* by Stephenie Meyer (2005)
- [ ] *Under the Lilacs* by Louisa May Alcott (1878)
- [ ] *The Wild Iris* by Louise Glück (1992)

Published in the United States by Clarkson Potter/
Publishers, an imprint of Random House, a division
of Penguin Random House LLC, New York.
clarksonpotter.com

CLARKSON POTTER is a trademark and POTTER
with colophon is a registered trademark of Penguin
Random House LLC.

ISBN 978-1-9848-2611-4

Printed in Malaysia

Book and cover design by Jessie Kaye

10 9 8 7 6 5 4 3 2 1

First Edition

THIS NOTEBOOK BELONGS TO

———————————————————————————————

Clarkson Potter/Publishers
New York

READING CHECKLIST

- [ ] *The Beet Queen* by Louise Erdrich (1986)
- [ ] *Blood Meridian* by Cormac McCarthy (1985)
- [ ] *Brick Lane* by Monica Ali (2003)
- [ ] *The Cardinal* by Henry Morton Robinson (1950)
- [ ] *Cherry* by Nico Walker (2018)
- [ ] *The Crimson Petal and the White* by Michel Faber (2002)
- [ ] *The Dream of the Red Chamber* by Cao Xueqin (1791)
- [ ] *The Flame Throwers* by Rachel Kushner (2013)
- [ ] *Harry Potter and the Goblet of Fire* by J.K. Rowling (2000)
- [ ] *A House of Pomegranates* by Oscar Wilde (1891)
- [ ] *The Last Song of Dusk* by Siddharth Dhanvant Shanghvi (2004)
- [ ] *Le Petit Chaperon Rouge* by Charles Perrault (1697)
- [ ] *My Name Is Red* by Orhan Pamuk (1998)
- [ ] *The Name of the Rose* by Umberto Eco (1980)
- [ ] *Red at the Bone* by Jacqueline Woodson (2019)
- [ ] *Red Sorghum* by Mo Yan (1987)
- [ ] *Rubyfruit Jungle* by Rita Mae Brown (1973)
- [ ] *The Salmon of Doubt* by Douglas Adams (2002)
- [ ] *The Scarlet Letter* by Nathaniel Hawthorne (1850)
- [ ] *When Hitler Stole Pink Rabbit* by Judith Kerr (1971)

Published in the United States by Clarkson Potter/
Publishers, an imprint of Random House, a division
of Penguin Random House LLC, New York.
clarksonpotter.com

CLARKSON POTTER is a trademark and POTTER
with colophon is a registered trademark of Penguin
Random House LLC.

ISBN 978-1-9848-2611-4

Printed in Malaysia

Book and cover design by Jessie Kaye

10 9 8 7 6 5 4 3 2 1

First Edition

THIS NOTEBOOK BELONGS TO

_____

Clarkson Potter/Publishers
New York

READING CHECKLIST

☐ *All the Light We Cannot See* by Anthony Doerr (2014)

☐ *The Chalk Man* by C. J. Tudor (2018)

☐ *City of Glass* by Paul Auster (1985)

☐ *Cloud Atlas* by David Mitchell (2004)

☐ *Fifty Shades of Grey* by E.L. James (2011)

☐ *Girl with a Pearl Earring* by Tracy Chevalier (1999)

☐ *Gray Mountain* by John Grisham (2014)

☐ *House of Sand and Fog* by Andre Dubus III (1999)

☐ *House of Stone* by Anthony Shadid (2012)

☐ *Invisible Man* by Ralph Ellison (1947)

☐ *The Lovely Bones* by Alice Sebold (2002)

☐ *Milkman* by Anna Burns (2018)

☐ *The Moonstone* by Wilkie Collins (1868)

☐ *The Shadow of the Wind* by Carlos Ruiz Zafón (2001)

☐ *The Silence of the Lambs* by Thomas Harris (1988)

☐ *Silver Sparrow* by Tayari Jones (2011)

☐ *The Snowy Day* by Ezra Jack Keats (1962)

☐ *White Teeth* by Zadie Smith (2000)

☐ *The White Tiger* by Aravind Adiga (2008)

☐ *The Wings of the Dove* by Henry James (1902)

Published in the United States by Clarkson Potter/
Publishers, an imprint of Random House, a division
of Penguin Random House LLC, New York.
clarksonpotter.com

CLARKSON POTTER is a trademark and POTTER
with colophon is a registered trademark of Penguin
Random House LLC.

ISBN 978-1-9848-2611-4

Printed in Malaysia

Book and cover design by Jessie Kaye

10 9 8 7 6 5 4 3 2 1

First Edition

THIS NOTEBOOK BELONGS TO

———————————————————————————

Clarkson Potter/Publishers
New York

READING CHECKLIST

- [ ] *All Among the Barley* by Melissa Harrison (2018)
- [ ] *Blonde* by Joyce Carol Oates (1999)
- [ ] *Crome Yellow* by Aldous Huxley (1921)
- [ ] *Cup of Gold* by John Steinbeck (1929)
- [ ] *Daisy Jones & The Six* by Taylor Jenkins Reid (2019)
- [ ] *Dandelion Wine* by Ray Bradbury (1957)
- [ ] *Doctor Marigold* by Charles Dickens (1865)
- [ ] *The Golden Apples* by Eudora Welty (1949)
- [ ] *The Goldfinch* by Donna Tartt (2013)
- [ ] *A Grain of Wheat* by Ngũgĩ wa Thiong'o (1967)
- [ ] *Half of a Yellow Sun* by Chimamanda Ngozi Adichie (2006)
- [ ] *In Search of the Canary Tree* by Lauren E. Oakes (2018)
- [ ] *Milk and Honey* by Rupi Kaur (2014)
- [ ] *Notes on a Banana* by David Leite (2017)
- [ ] *The Particular Sadness of Lemon Cake* by Aimee Bender (2010)
- [ ] *The Saffron Kitchen* by Yasmin Crowther (2006)
- [ ] *The Scent of Almonds and Other Stories* by Camilla Läckberg (2014)
- [ ] *Straw Dogs* by John Gray (2002)
- [ ] *The Temple of the Golden Pavilion* by Yukio Mishima (1956)
- [ ] *The Yellow House* by Sarah M. Broom (2019)

Published in the United States by Clarkson Potter/
Publishers, an imprint of Random House, a division
of Penguin Random House LLC, New York.
clarksonpotter.com

CLARKSON POTTER is a trademark and POTTER
with colophon is a registered trademark of Penguin
Random House LLC.

ISBN 978-1-9848-2611-4

Printed in Malaysia

Book and cover design by Jessie Kaye

10 9 8 7 6 5 4 3 2 1

First Edition